AF480046

INSECTS AND ARACHNIDS

ANIMAL BOOKS FOR KIDS

Children's Animal Books

Speedy Publishing LLC
40 E. Main St. #1156
Newark, DE 19711
www.speedypublishing.com

In just one square mile of any forest, there are more living creatures than there are humans on the whole Earth! Most of these critters are insects or arachnids. Let's find out more about them!

Beetle collection.

A WORLD OF INSECTS

There are more different types of insects than there are species of all other animals on our Earth. There are insects that mainly fly, like butterflies, moths, and, well, flies. There are insects like beetles and centipedes that mainly travel along the ground. There are grasshoppers that combine flying with jumping huge distances. And there are animals like bees, ants, and termites that are best described as social insects, no matter how they travel.

Insects are generally small, but some species can grow many inches long. A particular species, like cockroaches, may be much smaller in temperate areas like Europe than they are in tropical areas like Central America.

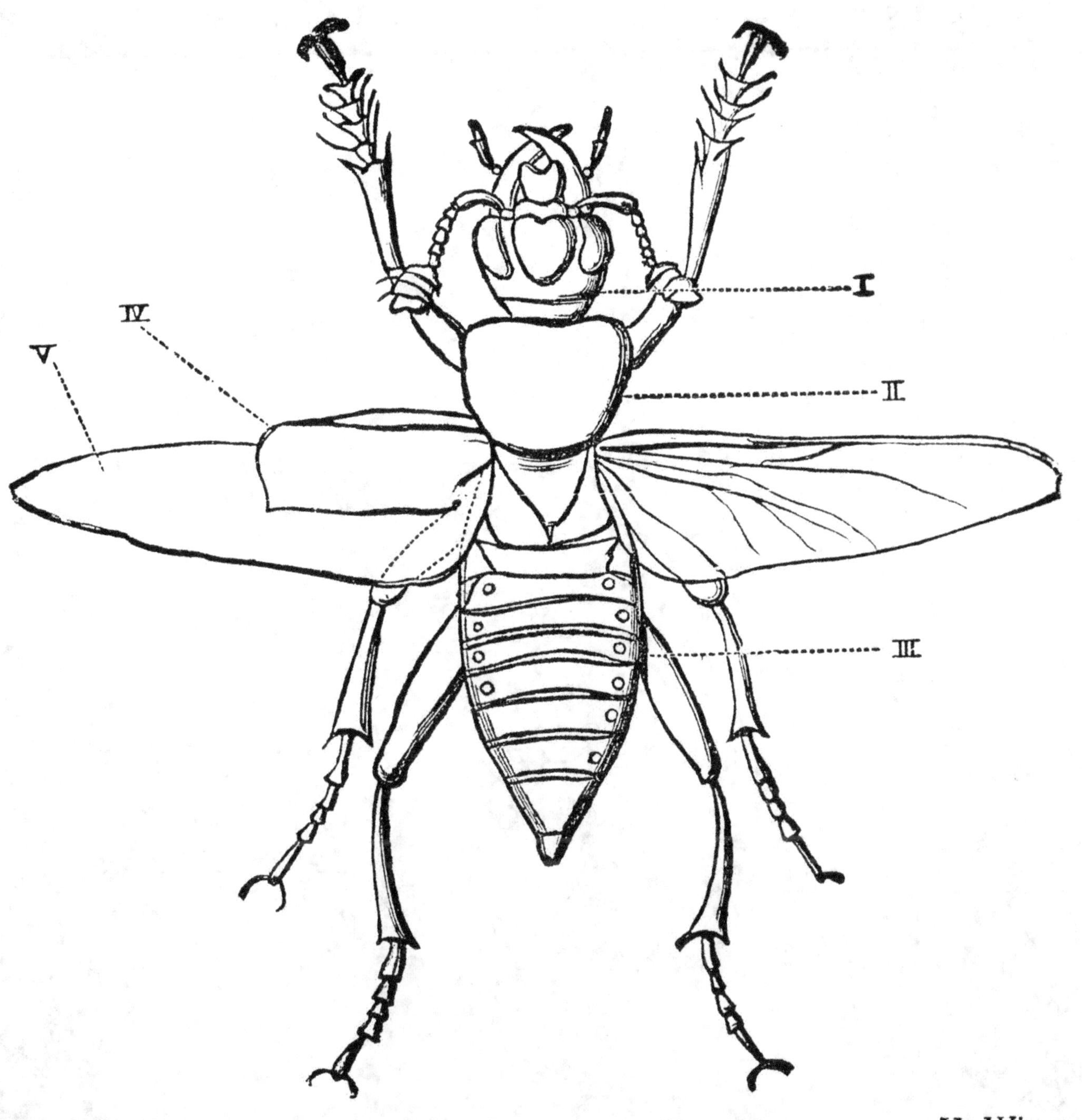

I. Head.   II. Thorax.   III. Abdomen.   IV. Wing-cases.   V. Wings.

Insects are successful because they can eat a wide range of foods, their exoskeletons are tough and protect them from a lot of damage, they are energy-efficient, and they lay lots and lots of eggs so their population grows even when a lot of young don't make it to adulthood.

Extreme magnification - Mosquito head, thin antennas.

Monarch Butterfly emerging from it's chrysalis.

WHAT MAKES AN INSECT?

Here are some features almost all insects have in common:

- They have a hard exterior shell. It is made of a material called chitin.

- Their bodies have three main segments: the head, the thorax, and the abdomen.

- They have at least two antennae on their heads, and six legs that emerge from their thorax. The legs are in three pairs.

- Some insects also have wings and can fly.

- Most insects lay eggs.

The structure of the beetle.

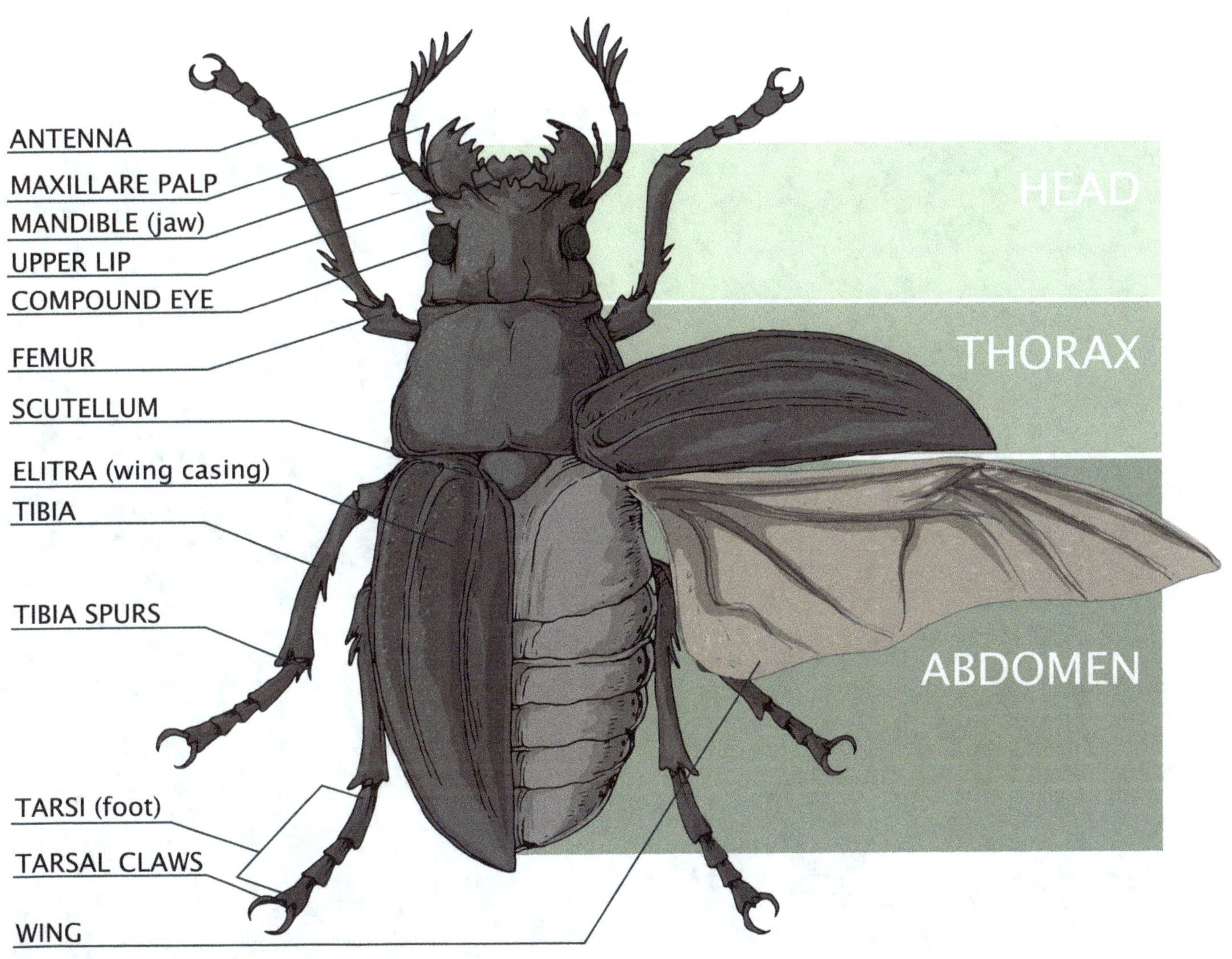

ANTENNA
MAXILLARE PALP
MANDIBLE (jaw)
UPPER LIP
COMPOUND EYE
FEMUR
SCUTELLUM
ELITRA (wing casing)
TIBIA
TIBIA SPURS
TARSI (foot)
TARSAL CLAWS
WING
HEAD
THORAX
ABDOMEN

Team of ants carry stick with chief on it.

CREEPY AND COOL INSECT FACTS

And here are some things to know about our insect friends and neighbors:

- The weight of all the ants in the world is greater than the weight of all the humans on Earth.

- Mosquitoes are more attracted to children than to adults, and to blondes more than to people with darker hair. Mosquitoes need nutrients from the blood they suck from your arm in order to produce eggs.

- A snail can survive up to three years between meals.

- A house fly, like one that buzzes you when you are trying to read a book in your house, lives about two weeks, unless you swat it first!

- A bee can travel up to 60 miles each day, mainly going out for pollen and bringing it back to the hive.

- An ant can carry loads as much as fifty times its own weight.

- When you hear crickets chirping, that's only the male crickets.

- Antarctica is the only continent that has no bees. In fact, in all of Antarctica, there is only one truly native insect species, a tiny midge which, although it belongs to the fly family, has no wings.

- Almost no insects live in Earth's oceans. This may be because their cousins the crustaceans have populated the niche in salt water that insects fill on land.

- Insects don't breathe through their mouths. They inhale and exhale through little holes, spircales, in their exoskeletons. And where animals use their blood system to deliver oxygen to cells and take away carbon dioxide, insects have a tracheal system, that takes care of gases separately. Their blood sort of flows around through the whole body without being organized into a system of veins and arteries. Their blood is mostly clear, with a greenish or yellowish tint.

- Insects were on Earth long before the dinosaurs. The oldest insect fossil we have found is over 400 million years old, twice as old as the oldest dinosaur fossil.

- Many insects have compound eyes made up of many *"Ommatidia"*. The ommatidia work together to give the insect a sort of mosaic image of what is around it. Dragonflies are the best-equipped in this area, with about 30,000 ommatidia per eye. Dragonflies and some other insects also have *"Ocelli"*, simple eyes, in between their main eyes. The ocelli can detect light and may help flying insects know where the horizon is.

Dragonfly in the morning dew.

- Most insects spend a relatively long time as larvae and pupae, and then just a few days or weeks as adults, able to reproduce. However, the queens of ant, bee, and termite colonies can live and lay their eggs for as much as thirty years, or even longer.

- The job of the queen of a colony of ants, wasps, bees, or termites is to produce eggs. They spend all day doing that, and the queen of a termite colony can lay up to seven thousand eggs a day.

Flying Lasius queen Ant portrait.

- Lots of insects have good hearing, but few have ears the way humans do. Their hearing sensors may be in their wings, on their necks, in their abdomens, or even in their mouths.

- Not all insects are *"bugs"*, although we use that term in English. Technically, a bug, a member of order Hemiptera, is an insect with a mouth-part like a needle. They use this mouth-part, or beak, to drink fluids from plants and animals—including from you and me!

Paper Wasp nest.

Black Scorpion about to prey on a bug.

NOT ALL ARACHNIDS ARE SPIDERS

Arachnids are not insects, although a lot of them look insect-like. The arachnids we know best are spiders, but other members of this group include scorpions and ticks. There are over 100,000 arachnids species on Earth.

WHAT MAKES AN ARACHNID?

Here are some things arachnids have in common:

- They have two major body sections, the prosoma (combining the head and the thorax) and the abdomen.

- They have eight legs, in four pairs. Each leg has seven segments.

- Some arachnids have chelicerae, which can work like jaws or fangs. They may also have pedipalps, which can act like antennae or crushing tools.

Tick.

- Some arachnids have chelicerae, which can work like jaws or fangs. They may also have pedipalps, which can act like antennae or crushing tools.

- They have simple eyes, not the compound eyes of insects.

- They have no antennae or wings.

- They do have a hard exoskeleton.

- Arachnids lay eggs.

- Most arachnids are predators, either hunting or trapping their prey. Some are venomous and can poison or paralyze the insects or even small animals they want to eat.

Close up of forest spider on cobweb after rain.

A WEB OF SPIDER FACTS

Of all the arachnids, we see and deal with spiders the most. Here are some things to know about our web-spinning friends:

- There are about a million spiders living in every acre of land, and as many as three million per acre in the tropics. Scientists say that humans are never more than ten feet away from the nearest spider!

- Spiders eat insects, pollinate plants, and process dead animals and plants so the Earth can absorb them. They are also an important source of food for many birds, fish, and small mammals.

- Every species of spider can spin silk, but not all spiders build webs. Spiders who build webs have claws at the end of each leg that they use to move around the web without getting stuck to it.

- Spiders don't have teeth. When they trap their prey, they inject digestive juices into it and wait until the juices have dissolved the inside of the insect or animal. Then they suck up their smoothie!

Spider Wrapping Prey in Web.

- Web-making spiders have as few as two and as many as six spinnerets at the back of the abdomen. Each spinneret has many holes and produces liquid silk that hardens in the air into strands. The spider has as many as seven different types of silk glands to produce different kinds of thread, with different amounts of stickiness and stretchiness.

- The name spider comes from an Old English word, *"Spithra"*, which means *"The Spinner"*. The word *"Spinster"*, meaning a woman who never marries, comes from the same source.

- The biggest spider species, the goliath spider, can grow almost a foot long and has one-inch fangs. It can hunt frogs, mice, birds, and even small snakes.

- Spider silk is very strong, five times stronger than a strand of steel of the same thickness.

The goliath birdeating spider

- A wolf spider can run as fast as two feet per second. A wheel spider gets away from danger by tucking in its legs and rolling away!

- Spider silk contains vitamin K. Before modern medicine, people used to put spider webs on cuts to stop the bleeding, and the vitamin K would help the wound heal more quickly.

Wolf spider in grass.

- Although most spider species are solitary, and individual spiders only meet others to mate, there are species of social spiders. Some colonies of spiders in Africa and India can cover trees, or even extend from tree to tree over a long distance.

- A spider can lay as many as three thousand eggs at a time. Most spider species don't care for their young, but wolf spiders carry their young on their backs until they are old enough and big enough to take care of themselves.

- Although most spiders only live about one year, some tarantulas can live as long as twenty years.

- If you have a spider in your house, catching it and letting it go outside does not help the spider. House spiders do not know how to survive outdoors.

There's lots more to learn about the tiny creatures who inhabit this Earth with us! Learn more in Baby Professor books like *Who Likes Bugs? We Do!* and *Discovering Winged Insects.*

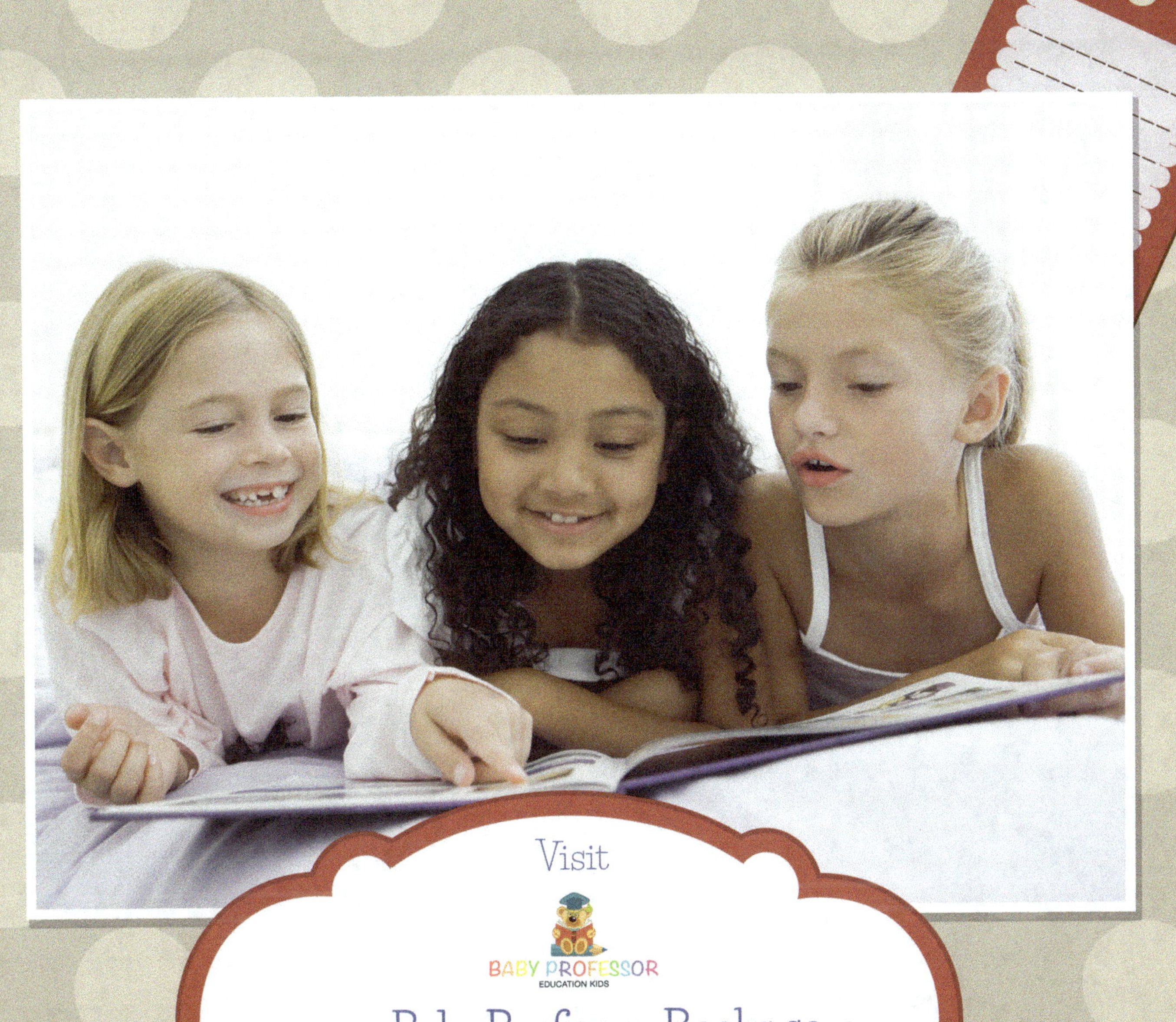

Visit

BABY PROFESSOR
EDUCATION KIDS

www.BabyProfessorBooks.com
to download Free Baby Professor eBooks
and view our catalog of new and exciting
Children's Books